Contact Information:

Email: Mindelevationforall@gmail.com

The Book About M.E. : Mind Elevation

© 2015 Chanekka Pullens. All Rights Reserved.

No part of this book may reproduced or transmitted in any form or by any means, written, electronic, recording, photocopying, or otherwise, without prior written permission of the author, Chanekka LuQuawn Pullens.

Books may be purchased in quantity and/or special sales by contacting the author by email at: Mindelevationforall@gmail.com , with "Book Purchase" in the subject line.

ISBN: 978-0-692-37911-0

1. Motivation 2. Inspiration

First Edition

Printed in the USA

THE BOOK ABOUT M.E.
:MIND ELEVATION

By:Chanekka Pullens

Dedicated to my mother, LaTonya Pullens, and in remembrance of my beloved big brother, Ke'Lonzo "Kenny" Pullens Sr.

"His mind is his treasure, that's buried deep in his conscience. He's to be what and who he's not destined to be. But who THEY want him to be. And for that he's unaware of his purpose."

-Chanekka Pullens

The mind is a terrible thing to waste. It is the most beautiful and useful component of the human race. You have the individual option of using your mind to change the face of the world. You have the individual option to change your mind.

The mind is the powerhouse of the body. The way you are able to control your mind determines the life you will live. If you exercise your mind to be able to reject and protect itself from negative influences, you will feel vast pride in having the strength to do so. But one has to take into account the term 'exercise' in my previous statement. You will not be able to have the strongest mind and will power overnight. Take for instance the great Dr. Martin Luther King Jr. or Malcolm X, even Ghandi. These great minds were established through will and exercise. Your mind can too, be an exceptional factor in changing the disadvantages of the nation, the world, or even just your life.

Negative circumstances and temptations surround us every day, everywhere, all the time. But the circumstances shouldn't necessarily determine your reaction. For your reaction will always determine the outcome, your outcome. One must remain aware that there are components that can influence the mind. Mental illness, mental disease and age. Yes! I testify that beyond these three reasons, there are none that should determine the way one can use their mind. A critic might ask, "What about race?" I will then ask, what race has the ability to control their mind more? White? Black? Asian? Though the skin vary in tones, the mind is a singular organ. Yes, it may differ in size and functions. One may find math easier than others. But what has that to do with Race? A critic might then ask, "What about geographic conditions?" I will then ask, a man who is raised in poverty doesn't have the same choice and freedom to use his mind as a white man raised in the suburbs? Granted, certain circumstances does derive from living in certain conditions. A man in poverty may be introduced to harsher environments and lifestyles. But the man in poverty has the ability to control his mind. To rise above the trap that has been placed to keep him and his brother down.

So no, race and geographic conditions does not determine the way one can use their mind. As previously stated, I believe through observations and discussions that mental illness, mental disease and age are the only factors that should oppress the strength of the mind. My most valued observation is through that of my own life.

Testimony

I was born on August 16, 1991 in Nashville, Tennessee to my mother Latonya Pullens and father Christopher Bell. At the time of my birth my mother was sixteen years old and my father was fifteen. My mother had already birthed a son, Kelonzo Pullens, who was born on July 10, 1990. And as math would concur my mother was fifteen at the time of his arrival. One could not imagine the numerous obstacles and disasters that my family would have to face throughout the years.

One of my first memories would have to be when my older brother Kenny and I was at the home of my great grandmother. I vividly recall us sitting on the floor watching "The Lion King", as I am around three and he is maybe four. I'm not sure why this particular memory decided to stay in my mind while others has vanished without a trace. As we were sitting, my father walked in and spoke with my mother before he helped me put on my jacket. I remember it being either pink or purple and made of a satin type fabric and puffy. Bubble-like. He proceeded to pick me up before we walked down a flight of stairs and pass a tall white gate that protected the pool. I know that my father fastened me into my car seat that held its position directly behind the driver. I can recall us driving down the street with lights and signs glazing and shining brightly. He was taking me to McDonalds, this I know, but I don't remember turning into the parking lot or anything afterwards that night.

The next memory that I would have of my father would be the last. I remember that I am four years old in 1995 and the church was our location. I remember a lot of people mourning, even a person or two walked outside. I was sitting beside my mother I believe, before being interrupted when someone grabbed me. I'm not sure who it was or why they thought it was this great idea to hold me over my father's casket. My mother tells me that I was telling my father to wake up and that I wanted to take a nap with my daddy. Until this day, I remember looking down onto my father's corpse. I have the slightest clue why this particular memory has made its permanent imprint onto my memory. But it has. And many nights and days, I remember looking down.

One would assume that the life of a four year old would get better after she buried her father. He was only twenty years old. It haunts me to know that his murder was premeditated. Planned. Thought about step by step. Deliberate. As he stepped from his vehicle one night outside his mother's home. Boom! Gone. Bullet to his cranium. Executed. I can never imagine my grandmother who was maybe steps away, having to discover her baby, lifeless in the street. Like an animal. Like nothing. All because of jealousy. Granted, my father made a choice to live a life where there are only two real outcomes. I'm sure that he was aware of the consequences of his actions. But nobody ever thinks that it would be them. You know. How could you? Why would you?

Throughout the following years I would be blessed with four more siblings, brothers to be specific. On April 1, 1997 my mother would give birth to her sixth and final child. Yep, in seven years my dear mother had given birth to six children beginning at fifteen years old. There is a lot of stress and responsibility that comes with having that many children in poverty. Over the course of the years, we would inevitably be divided. Three were 'taken' (and I use that term loosely and strongly simultaneously) while three of us stayed. Kenny, Seneca (the baby), and I stayed with our mother while William and Devonta went to live with their grandparents. D'tearius eventually went to live with his aunt for a few years before my mother regained custody of him.

Leading up to 2001, my family had: lost our home when my youngest brother's father robbed a gun store and brought everything back to our house; which resulted in us being evicted and homeless. He was also the person that shot my mother in the leg. I was young but I remember my mother lying on the front porch bleeding out. I remember the ambulance and its lights. I remember crying in the living room in the arms of one of her 'friends'. Next, another home had burned down with everything in it. Kenny and I had to be brought home from school by a teacher only to see it gone to the ground, all physical memories were now ash. Also, Kenny and I had to go into a foster care system and went through roughly three families in maybe six months. But it wasn't because no other family would take us in after six months, it's because we were back with my mother. After going through so much pain and misery, she remained strong and did what was needed and required to get her children back, instead of just leaving us there as she could of. And I will forever be thankful to the woman I call my mother for that. We also went through our first awful tornado. My mother was gone and Kenny and I had to hide in the closet for what seemed like forever. Thank God my mother was safe, but our only place of fun was destroyed. The joys of living in the projects, one park. When the park was gone imagination came into play even more. My brothers and I would build forts with sheets in our room and sometimes we would climb on the gate that protected the electrical unit. One day Kenny got caught on it, and it ripped through his flesh from his wrist up his arm maybe five inches. I remember seeing meat and bone which made me terrified. There was even a time when Kenny and I had to go live with my uncle, his wife and two kids for a while. But finally, the move to Knoxville, Tennessee was in July of 2001.

 I remember so vividly the beginning, I would sit on the porch with no friends, until one day I saw her. I'm not sure why she is the only person from my childhood that I remember perfectly every detail. She was tall and had a caramel complexion and on this day she wore a pink plaid outfit. We would be introduced and she would become my first childhood friend in Knoxville, Tennessee. Her name is Myiesha Diana Gillette, born May 16, 1990. You can basically say that we were in the same boat. The life of the projects and her family was sort of like mine. Her mother too had six children, but they were all girls and one boy, as opposed to my mother's five boys with me as the only girl.

Time would tear us apart, but more time would bring us right back together. She gave birth to her first child when she was fourteen, Domisha, and she was my light and reason for smiles. She was the first baby that I'd been introduced to since birth, babysat, and took part in raising. A few years later Myeisha would give birth to her second child, Jamira, as a teenager. Between us two, over the years, we would: skip school, smoke weed, go see boys, and be reckless. We would get into trouble and not care or think about the consequences. This immature and relentless time would bring her two children and trapped into the statistics. And well me, my first love and heartbreak. We were both fourteen years old when we lost our virginity on Father's day. I think as he opened my legs I thought that it had some kind of significance because of my father 'situation'. If only has was able to tell me "NO! Not yet". I would have proudly obliged.

The year I lost my Chaste would also be the year I would be reintroduced to the world of death. I recall him being poorer than the others. He talked with a slight slur through his teeth and he was uniquely different. He was passionate about literature, very energetic and had obtained a happy soul through his shortcomings. Our peers would make fun of him daily by pointing, laughing, and degrading him for being unique. But me, I enjoyed him. His energy was captivating, and he was a very sweet and sincere young boy. The day before we made the trip I asked him to borrow a pencil and he handed me a black mechanical pencil with a red stem. I have never used that pencil since that day and it remains in my infamous memory box.

It was April 30, 2004; I remember it so perfectly that it's almost scary. We were to hike a trial a few miles that eventually would lead us to a beautiful waterfall. We are all in the 8th grade, excited that our middle school careers were almost over. After this summer we would be in high school, the big leagues. Throughout the hike our peers would continue to make fun of him, as it being a natural part of their day. I remember as we entered the presence of the waterfall, he stopped and grabbed a 2 liter soda from his backpack, then he was gone. I was playing in the water, enjoying the moment, when all the commotion commenced. I saw him struggling and panicking to stay afloat, trying and wanting to save his life. A teacher and a student leaped into the water to try to save him. Unfortunately, his placement was inches from where the waterfall crashed into the lake, so the pressure was powerful. I saw him go under and come back up, before going under without rising. I couldn't believe for a moment what had happened. This was the first time I've ever witnessed someone lose their life right in front of me. To someone many called names but I called a friend, and I would tell people to leave him alone. I promise, that I never once called him anything other than his name. Christopher Drinkard.

We were all rushed back to the bus, having to walk the miles through the hiking trial seemed like it took hours. The teacher and older student were trying frantically to contact help with their radios, without a good signal in the trees. Once we were back on the bus we sat silent for what seemed like days, unaware of the outcome of my dear friend. Hours passed before we received the report, that he had been pinned against a rock by the current. He was feet below the surface directly under the waterfall when his soul was called home. They cried because they knew that they had made his short sweet life miserable. I cried because they had made his life miserable, and that he could finally be free. The drive back to Knoxville seemed like twice the time that it took to get there. We pulled into the back of Vine Middle School and parked in front of the cafeteria. All of our loved ones were gathered there upon our arrival. Parents, siblings, teachers, packed into this space, crying, afraid. Everyone ran into the arms of their dearly loved, me into my mother graces, and cried. At home I cried and months later, tears would still fall.

His funeral was held in this huge church, "Tabernacle" if I'm not mistaken. It was filled with those consumed with regret and those who truly loved him and his spirit. I looked onto his corpse, remembering the last time I was in this position I was four years old looking down onto my father. He wore the sharpest off white suit that I ever seen, even until this day. His father and younger brother ensemble was the exact replica. He had a beautiful home going service. This was the first event that I became depressed. For some odd reason, Usher's "Burn" would do a number on me every time I would listen to it. Even now, that is Chris's song to me.

One would not believe that amount of death I would encounter after the first. It would make one's head spin, and an exorcism wasn't too far-fetched to help deal with the amount of emotion involved. In May 2006, DeSean Jarrell Garner would be killed by a former classmate in the street. I remember seeing him run down the hallways and just be his silly self. After his death I recall the blood that stained the site on which his life was taken. He was 18. In October 2006, Brooke M. Calloway Moore, would lose her battle to Pontine Glioma, a brain tumor which she was diagnosed with one year prior. I remember her being so stunningly gorgeous and active. From running track with us, to cheering and modeling. I was so confused as to how someone as amazing and brilliant as her could become victim of such illness. She was 15. In 2007, Brandon Martin was shot in the neck while participating in a drive by. The last time I saw him was the day before his death.

He was sitting on the porch next door to mine, alone. He wore all brown and told me to come give him a hug. I said "No" and continued walking, and the next time I would see him would be in his casket. He was 21. Or what about Mike Mike Cowen and his girlfriend Brittany, at their home when someone came in to rob them. Stabbed this beautiful young woman numerous times and shot him dead, to possess what they possessed. Marcus Carmicheal, a young man I've known since elementary, trying to rob someone while in their car. The man drove away and pinned Marcus against the pole and the car. He was 16. Then there's Kevin Smith, a knock at the door, as he opened it, Boom! A shot to the head. He too was 16. Gang affiliation.

    Baltimore was shot in the head by a sixteen year old boy. I remember this man, who lived a building from mine. I recall this night as it was raining when I heard a shot. It was a sound that had become so natural and a part of my life that I would not jump nor budge. I walked down the street only to see Baltimore lying on the ground with his brains being washed by the rain. Someone held an umbrella over him as to preserve his thoughts. But they along with his soul would forever be a memory to those who called him family or a friend. Ryan Anthony McDonald, was shot while sitting in the cafeteria at a high school. And Micheal Theron Gillette, was dragged almost 100 feet while hanging outside a truck window; when he was finally released the back tires ran over his head. He was allegedly making a drug deal that went wrong. Finally, Justin Walker, the star basketball player of my high school who was killed in a car accident.

For years I allowed anger and resentment to control my heartbeat. I allowed the struggle and system to control me and my mind. Don't get me wrong the only damage I created was to myself. I damaged my mind and my body. But just as it was easy to allow my negative circumstances to control my life, it was even easier to absorb the positive entities in life. Ironically enough it was through a book. Even more ironically it was through my book; my journal. One day while reading it I had an epiphany. You're living an uneasy life because you have been living an uneasy life. Get it? From the liquor and marijuana to the sex and deceit. I had been living an uneasy life. I must admit, it wasn't all bad, and although I lived in poverty, I am satisfied with my childhood overall. I noticed that it's not until your innocence has been taken that you begin living a guilty life.

These deaths are all connected to me personally. These were all souls that I had the grace of knowing and their lives would not go unnoticed. Take note that I am in no way placing blame on them. Just stating that a different path could have been taken. But unfortunately the majority of these lives had minds and had the freedom to control their lives. Either they made the decision to be a part of the gang, rob that person, sell that drug, or choose that battle. We are all aware of the consequences of our actions. We all have those "if I'd known then what I know now" moments and events. This is a chain of life that has to decrease, but instead it is proliferating at an absurd rate. These lost lives were in my neighborhood, in a small town of one area in Knoxville, Tennessee. And this isn't all of them! Not even half. Now, let's back up on the scale and imagine this on a national or global bases. It is absolutely scary to know that such destiny has become a common norm in society. We must unite to recreate the common norm and what is expected.

The future is determined by what present steps are taken. We cannot and should not depend solely on the political sphere. But there is enough power, if united, to elect responsible and honest political leaders. Instead we allow the greed and selfish driven leaders to remain in control. Individuals whom we can't trust or rely on to promote our "best" interest. Because we don't speak and vote as we should. It pains me to hear the young say that they don't vote. Or what does their one vote matter. But that is what has been accepted and expected. I say, NO! Who has that much of a right and power to dictate the life I choose to live. We must band together for our children. Vote and elect individuals with pure and uncorrupted hearts and minds to bring forth equality. To bring forth fairness and a chance to the children and generations that so rightfully deserves it. It can happen, change can happen. We just have to come together with the faith and belief that it can. Once this becomes understood, it will create a chain reaction and it will be more accepted. This new standard will replace the current system and more lives will be changed for the better, not destroyed.

Mind elevation. You must take control of your mind. Give your mind the chance to be exceptional. Give you the chance to be remarkable. You don't have to be the smartest or the prettiest to have a beautiful mind. And no, you don't have to become perfect to use your mind to its fullest potential. For no human is. But you must have absolute control over your own thoughts. Your own dreams. You must keep a tight grasp of your own destiny. Because this world will take your bright destiny and turn your life into darkness. If you let it. If you control your mind, you control a fraction of the world. And you gain the ability to allow it to multiply.

You may be lost, confused, and afraid to step towards greatness. But always keep in mind that the greatest steps worth taking will sometimes be the hardest first steps to take. Remain focused, dedicated, strong, and self-aware. Stay focused on the goal, dedicated to the journey, strong throughout the obstacles and self-aware of your ability to achieve all the above and beyond. Regardless of all the "No's" and "You cant's" that the world tells you and that you may sometimes tell yourself. I guarantee the moment you silence the doubt of the world and the doubt in yourself, you will sense a weight lifted from your back. You will begin to appreciate your mind and your ability far more. And once that happens, once you begin to speak up for your beliefs and conquer your fears. You will control the fraction of the world that is yours and you'll love it!

Points to Ponder

-
-
-
-
-
-
-
-
-
-
-
-

The Brother

In our modern society the mind is wasted and ignorance is appreciated and accepted. It is celebrated in our world when a brother murders his brother because they were birthed by different mothers. Why must our young black men be denied the opportunity to achieve greatness? Be denied, to study a cell from imprisonment instead of through a microscope in a lab? Why must it be stereotypical that we as the black race be inferior and inadequate? I shall speak and say that my brother is NOT beneath the world although they continue to live in hell. Why must we continue to be denied the chance of a good life, as our fathers before us had? It appears to be a cycle that only a few is willing to break. The few that embraces the potential of their mind and reject the doubt of the world. But why must there only be a few? A few isn't enough to protect the survival of our future generations. The solution? Many. Many can come together to pave a righteous road for our successors. Successors that will succeed from our success, or fail from our failures.

We must gain the confidence and strength needed to overpower the negative influences. We must become open minded so that we may be able to practice the words that we speak of. Why would my child or my little brother obey and understand from watching, not to touch that bottle when my skin and breath smell of toxic. Or could I expect my baby cousin not to give birth to a child, until her wall holds a diploma, while I carry my child on my hip. We cannot speak one thing with our mouths while doing the opposite with our bodies. So practice before you preach. And overcome before you lead. The cycle of greatness will begin to spread, just as the cycle of weakness. Give our children the option and chance to learn from our mistakes. As I learned from my mother. As she had her first child at fifteen, yet I am twenty-three without experiencing my first. Or how hard it is to live in this world without receiving a proper education. My mother was not able to graduate high school because of her circumstances, yet I am less than ten classes away from receiving my Bachelors Degree. This is a testimony that it is possible. But we must act now. My mother constantly told me that I was beautiful and smart. So when a man spoke of my beauty I had no need to fall in love with his view of me. Because I already knew of my beauty, because my mother told me daily. If she hadn't, who's to say that I would become attracted to every man that told me so. How many statistics would I of became? How many children would I of birthed? How many projects would I have lived? Only my Lord knows. But my mother, a single women and through her experiences, created me. Created this woman. These words, this wisdom, this hope and burning passion in me.

  Now, if one woman can change the life of one child. Image what thousands of women can do to inspire thousands of children. To give thousands of young boys and girls hope and a choice. Teach your child the right way. My boyfriend constantly says "who's to say". Exactly, who's to say what is right and wrong. Society? But what isn't right is young men getting buried into nature without seeing adulthood, or women getting buried into statistics and losing hope. That isn't right, and this I know beyond a reasonable doubt. I'm tired of witnessing young mothers allowing their young baby to curse at her or speak the words that comes from the mouth of an adult. She laughs, not aware of the man she is creating. Another brother who will have two inevitable outcomes for his life. Death or jail. Because he was raised to think that is okay to curse openly and proudly, and gets kicked out of school. Forced to turn to the streets, sell drugs, or find comfort and peace in a gang. If only, his mother or father would of told him to stop. Told him "No, don't say that word". Held a stern foot and strong mind instead of laughing him into a disastrous future.

  All the souls that was lost within a few short years of my life. All the young men that was trapped and lost, had something in common. Anger and resentment. Rather it was towards another person or himself. Enough to conclude to rob that person or join that gang. Even the ones that fell victim to the gun that was held by another. The one who held the weapon had a dark cloud, enough to allow him to pull the trigger to take that soul. As they continue to breath after they'd taken a life, they too are lost, afraid, and a victim. Of hopelessness, of someone not telling him "No", take a better road and make a better life. Instead the sphere and circle of life and death continues. Now, the victim that has breath is incarcerated for life, or half of it. A young dream and hope, trapped. In a system that was created to keep him there. With no hope and chance of redemption. Because he wasn't given the chance of someone encouraging him to elevate his mind above the temptations and circumstances.

How is it that he is so angry at his brother, because he decides to wear a different color, or live on a different street? It is preposterous and monstrous that this is our reality. The fact that it is an increasing trend, symbolizes no hope for our future. Gang members are getting younger and younger at the time of initiation. We have so much potential as not only a race, but as people to do so much more. To progress so much further. We are crippled by the standards and perceptions of society by a different race. The white man is so quick to speak on our race with little respect and regard to the fact that we too are human. We too have the ability to achieve greatness. They may have the idea, but we are giving them satisfaction to the outcome in which they desire. Our failure. But me for one refuse to fail and allow them to smile as I bury my brother. Laugh as they ride by my sister catching the bus to the welfare office with a stroller and another child at her side.

I believe that we will prevail, because we are a race of greatness that have been lost in time. Lost in planned destruction and deception. Lost in the ideals and ideas of the white man. The "White Power", or so they think. I for one say stand!

Stand for your right to live a good life, and a life worth living. A life that can contribute to the growth of the people, instead of the demise thereof. Prove those who deny you the will wrong, and show that you can. You do NOT have to be the intended and expected outcome of your situation. I was born and raised in poverty and I witnessed the death and loss of many. Just as many as I've buried, I've seen far more go into the endless sphere of the prison system, and become addicted to incarceration. Addicted, to the fact they have no place in a "free" society. And yes, I use free as loosely as possible. For we are far from "free", but we're also far from being destroyed and hopeless. Far from the point of no return. Far from where we came before the Civil Rights Movement. Or are we?

Poetic Justice

Educate, don't hate.

We all eat from the same plate.

Placed at the bottom in the dirt, just because of my race.

My tone is evil, inferior, I'm peasantry

21st century and slavery is still my destiny.

Chains trap me to my past

That surpasses my years here.

Why must the greatest blessing of 'creation' be my greatest fear?

Will my seed, be seen, as "something" less to demean.

Will he be judged before he speaks, walks, even breathe.

Will he be killed by his brother, that didn't come from me?

Or entrapped in the trap that was placed for him to be.

Will he desire only money or addicted to what makes all funny.

Mary will he carry? Will it be the reason I bury, my seed

Because I've seen it with my mother's seed.

Only 23, 6 feet, is where he be.

So much potential and hope was in my big brother, in all my brothers.

When will this curse break?

When will respect for each other be respected, not neglected

They say the truth be naked.

Yet, lies bare, everywhere

Yet, the truth is covered, the shy sheep in wolves skin

Truth portrayed as wrong

Truth delayed so long

But the lies, won't last for long. My nephews will be aware

His young friends, he'll share.

They will be raised by truth, is my dream, and

I'll start from there.

Points to Ponder

-
-
-
-
-
-
-
-
-
-
-
-

The Goddess

A queen inherits her throne, rather she believes in her kingdom or not. The power and beauty is passed down from birth. Once you take your first breath, another queen has risen. Once you take your first step, a queen has embarked on her journey. And once a queen falls, her true self will be revealed. Either she will rise back up, take another step, and continue her legacy. She will empower those whom she embraces, rather a king or queen. Empower them to rise back up, and continue their destiny. And this will become the cycle of the goddess. She will brush the figs from her gown, wipe the tears from her eyes, and continue her destiny, with strength and dignity. Or, she will physically rise, leaving behind her mind. She will become content, on serving the world for their amusement. She will begin to lose control of her, because she has lost control over her own mind. That who controls the mind, controls the body, and through her body, her life will be controlled.

So with the world controlling her body, she will fall victim to despair. Victim, to those who only want her body and the victim to herself with no mind. No mind to remind her of her destiny, her journey, or her kingdom. To remind her of her potential of greatness, her potential of enrichment. Yet, she will become engulfed in the idea of what others has portrayed her to be. She will begin to live a life, which is not hers. If you're not living for yourself, a life that is yours, why live?

Queens! We must stop degrading our temples and our livelihoods. We must become more accepting and respectful to our bodies. We are all temples of the Lord and we must treat our bodies with dignity and respect. We must be kind and loving to our bodies. Be proud of your blessing, for your body regardless of tone and shape is a true blessing. We should carry ourselves as we would desire our daughters to carry themselves. Be knowledgeable to our self-worth and appreciative of how much we have to offer.

We as women are the key to humanity, the reason for recreation. Yet, these facts are unappreciated as to the lack of knowledge of how important child birth is. So many of our youth are having numerous kids before they turn a reasonable age. They're not aware of the impact that it will have on not only themselves but society as a whole. Raising a child at the age of fourteen is so approved in today's world, that it is absolutely horrifying. I mean just ask yourself, "How many young girls are parents that you know?" Me, try more than half of my high school graduating class. More than a quarter were mothers before we even walked across the stage.

I am nobody to judge, so trust that I am not. I am just speaking on the facts of our current reality. All the children birthed by these young girls are blessings and Gods most precious gift. But we must be reminded that these children are our future. We can raise them to be better and recreate our nation, and one day the world. It all starts now, with these children; these vessels that deserve all the good the world has to offer. We must instill in them, the lessons we've learned. The importance of knowledge and acceptance with their bodies. I'm going to talk about mainly our daughters in reference to the "queens" topic.

At a young age, children are so easily influenced and impressionable. Baby girls look up to their mothers with a sense of innocence. They have no knowledge of what their mother is doing is right or wrong. They only see and react. They become, in a sense, what they are surrounded in. Granted, once they come to a reasonable age, they will take the path that is theirs. But that choice is greatly influenced by her mother.

Testimony

I previously mentioned the location where I was raised, but never the place where I was raised. I remember attending Green Magnet School in the 5th grade. My teacher was Mr.Wrushen and he stood with a tough frame. He drank coffee every day and I never understood why. But I remember him being a tough man and passionate about teaching. Whenever any student acted out of line, he had no issues with grabbing the paddle. For that, I behaved.

After school, I would walk down this hill before coming to the street that connected Green School to Austin Holmes. I recall Mr.Gun, the crossing guard that assisted us in crossing the street. He was the sweetest man and good at his job. Once down the hill you were officially in my hood. Austin Holmes was a fun place for the most part when innocence was present. My friends and I would ride bikes down past Magnolia, play kickball, freeze tag, etc. Just enjoying life without many worries. The best part was the center that was placed right by the mailboxes. We would go every day after school to unwind. There was basketball, video games, foosball, and a place where you could do homework. One of my favorite things was creating squares with pretty string.

Every Saturday morning, there was this Sunday school truck that came and parked in front of the mailboxes. They would lay two blue tarps down on each side of the sidewalk. One side was for girls, the other was for the boys. They would teach a biblical lesson and we would have interactive games where we could win toys and candy. Almost every child from the neighborhood would attend. And we would all leave with a toy or the treat for the day. One day during the week the owners of the truck would walk around the neighborhood and give us a paper with a biblical quote on it. It would also contain the treat that would be given out at the end of the lesson. I think the start time was 10am. I'm not too sure on that fact, but I would wake up every Saturday morning with Kenny, get dressed, and walk down to the mailboxes. When Seneca became old enough, he too would begin to attend.

This would continue for a few years, before stopping. I remember the times when things would begin to change for the worse. Forever changing my friends and our environment. One day the center was up, the next it was demolished. One day we were full of innocence and happiness. The next it was guilt and anguish. Gangs and violence took over as if peace was never present. Through Vine Middle all the way to Austin East, there would be constant change for the worse. This was a vital time that would determine the path in life you would take. Many of my childhood friends are deceased, in jail for many years, lost in the world, and a few doing great.

Those deceased, imprisoned, or lost took a path that they were peer pressured into, just fell into, or other reasons beyond my knowledge. But the few that's doing good went off to college and refused not to be limited to the Knoxville gates. I wish our center was never destroyed utmost because that was the pivotal point. With nothing positive left, only negative remained; as if the fall of my generation was inevitable. I say that through this time, I managed and survived because of family. I fell into my path because of the love I have for my mother.

My mother has always been strong willed and strong minded. I understand now as an adult that everything she has ever done to me would be a crucial factor in who I am today. Then, as a reckless teenager, I never understood that only love and concern influenced her actions. I would be put on punishment, but sneak out and stay gone. I would go over Myiesha house, which was my second home, and get lost. Not worried about the consequences of when I would see my mother again. This would continue until I came of age to understand and realize my potential. The potential to help my mother and my family's name. I've always been wise beyond my years, giving advice to my mother friends before I experienced their issues. I guess that wisdom is why I'm typing these words now.

Now, keep in mind that my mother and I haven't always been on the best of terms. I had anger built up along with confusion all in one body. So, my attitude was mean and my mother was my victim. I've always loved her and never once have I cursed at my mother. But I hurt her worse with my attitude alone, and even through it she loved me and remained content in caring for my well-being. I could have easily went down the path of many others that I grew up with. I could have allowed myself to become limited to the gates of Knoxville because I had many chances. But the influence, guidance, and love of my mother lead me to my destiny.

    So to the goddess, remember you are a blessing with a purpose. You must be able to control your mind to fulfill your destiny. Be the queen that you were created to be and live a righteous life. Live a life where you can influence others, so that when your physical components has become one with the earth, your purpose and name will be spoken through generations. If you need help during the journey. Ask. As I say, it's as easy for the prideful rich man to fall with no help, than a wise poor man to rise with it.

Puppet Master

Most of us are controlled by the puppet master.

  Brains, I can't have one.

  Beauty, I must create.

  Hours spent, money wasted

To change my imperfections.

  Butt injections, the bigger the better,

Natural and real doesn't matter.

As long as men stare and lust

  In men we're taught to trust.

 To be or not to be,

A stereotypical black woman.

Only meaningful words I can speak to

  A man is "I'm coming".

Afterwards, he leaving

  While I'm fixing my weave and

Looking in the mirror, I see the invisible strings.

Puppet Master,

    Controlling my movements

To be accepted by the cruel men

    And women that judge

    As if they sit above.

    The world, it's so cold

Role models can only rap and remove a thong,

Rap and dance to the beat, but on the inside they're just as hollow

As long as money follows

Self-respect and pride is swallowed.

The root of evil isn't money

Its greed, power, and self-importance.

It's the need to be seen as indestructible and immortal.

As I remind you, that your heartbeat is as temporary as the weak

… Minds, self-esteem

For pride, confidence, and knowledge will prevail.

So, to the puppet master,

Controlling her mind now, in time you will fail.

She will cut the strings, begin to believe in the

    True beauty that is naturally instilled.

Footprints of the strong and brave

Has been empty for so long, but soon filled.

So enjoy your moment, puppet master.

Points to Ponder

-
-
-
-
-
-
-
-
-
-
-

When one is released from jail what options do they have when they must mark "felon" on their job application? To be denied as they always had. Because of a mistake and choice that they made when they were five, ten, even twenty years younger. Rarely does the employer take into account that they are human who sometimes deserves a second chance. Who are trying to live a better life after being incarcerated for countless years. I see it so much when felons have the door slammed in their face and backs turned on them because of their "label". A label that will follow them throughout their lives.

But they deserve a second and third chance. For those who deny them their opportunities is a man. A man who is not labeled "Perfect" and has no right to deny someone the right to become a part of society. Yes, some crimes are far worse than others. A man who rapes and murders a woman should not be free from imprisonment, for that punishment is still unjust. But a man who is forced to serve twenty years and become a felon for smoking marijuana and growing the plants. To be released and treated as if he'd assassinated Kennedy or Lincoln. That is not only unjust but unfair and unacceptable. If someone who is a felon is trying and making an effort to find honest work even go back to school. They should be allowed to do so because they deserve that chance.

Within the time of imprisonment, they are sometimes able to think of the wrong they've done and desire to make it right. They've had time to elevate their mind and restructure their mental process and functions. Sometimes that is all that is needed, time. Time to just think and understand what has occurred. How you have gotten to this place and how you will prevent others from making the same mistakes. Even if it is just children on the street in your neighborhood, talk to them, share with them the importance of living a good and "free" life. How vital it is for them to leave that gang behind and put that gun down. To go back to school and graduate. Share with them how they can benefit and help heal humanity. Ensure them that they are important and that they matter. Tell them to just stop and think before they make life changing and sometimes life ending decisions. Sometimes all it needs to do is be heard. Press the importance of an education above all.

   The deliberate lack of education for our children is the new form of slavery. When a child receives no education, there are not many options that can be rewarding. He will only be able to work at low paying jobs with basically no benefits. Be forced to turn to the street life. Gangs, selling drugs, and inevitably death or jail. Then the cycle will continue. Be endless and become all we know, all our children know, until we are again, inferior. So we must protect our potential and our destiny. We must protect the ability and strength of our minds. We must protect our children. I refuse to allow my nephews to be raised in a world where the current state of his race be the only. For them to fall victim of what is "expected" by the "superiors".

Entrapment

Negativity is one of the easiest things to be absorbed in. It can take control of your inner energy and transform you into a negative minded individual. It is easy to be consumed by negative actions and thoughts, thus creating negative situations. Therefore, it is the negative situation that we must be able to control. This particular objective is far more complex than simply controlling your mind. With controlling a negative event, you must be able to envision a positive outcome and solution. Once you have a positive aspect in mind, you will be more willing to make that vision come to life. For example, if you are unemployed and are days away from being evicted you could become a victim of that negative situation and allow it to determine your life. Or you could think of what positive outcomes could derive from this situation. Maybe you could contact temp services, ask management for an extension or even be responsible and pack your belongings. Even if you must go into a shelter until you are able to get work and find a new home. Remain positive that you will prevail through this negative state and you will be proud and satisfied that you were strong through it. You will be thankful that you learned from the mistakes that got you into the situation in the first place.

Negative minded individuals can also cause you to fall victim. You must separate yourself from this negative minded person and venture off onto your own positive path. I understand that sometimes it isn't as easy to leave all negative minded people behind, mainly some family members. But if you are able to strengthen your mind to the point where no one can influence and impact your mind and life. You can be in the same room with those individuals without being affected by their negativity. Be strong and self-aware of the consequences. You would have put in such an effort to get your mind to this point; nobody deserves or has that right to take your most prized possession from you, your mind.

It is easier said than done, granted, but practice makes perfect. You will not be able to achieve this great achievement overnight. But you must maintain the power and will to do so. You must not allow others to determine the path and actions that you take in life. Each of us has our own lives to live. We all have one chance to make it count for the better. Don't allow yourself to live for another person. Don't allow anyone to have such power to control the thoughts of you. The destiny you will have in this life is the destiny that you create yourself. You can choose to pull that trigger, or rob that store, or sell that drug. There are circumstances that you may find yourself in that isn't your choice. If someone was robbing your home with a malicious intent, and you are face to face with the weapon in your hand. Should you allow someone to flee that came to bring you and your family harm? I'm not here to say to kill that person in self-defense, or to hold him there until the police come. That decision should be based on what you think is best for you and your family. But before a decision is produced, you must ask yourself, will you be able to live with such consequences.

The world really is what you make it. Many people may disagree, but you can and must create the world that you want in your mind. If you want to live a positive life you must believe that it can exist. Because as you can see, you cannot believe in something by simply existing in this world; for it is a harsh and cold one. There are many evil people in this world that will take you for granted and take advantage of all the goodness you have to offer, solely to allow themselves to advance. So you must become knowledgeable and aware of the tricks and deceptions that they will use to trap you. Knowledge is the key to breaking generations' worth of curses and lies. We must teach our children our past so that they will learn from our mistakes. So that they will reject the lies we were told and taught to believe.

We must also teach them to not fall; but stand together to make this world a place where we can all be united. I know that someone is thinking, "Why now, after centuries will we become united?" or "Why now, will we accept a race other than our own?" I will say because patience is the key to any virtue. Over thousands of years, there has been judgment and resentment. Anger and hatred towards those who are different because we have been taught and manipulated to believe so. Now, we must reverse these unjust teachings. Now, we must instill in our future leaders that unity and respect is the way of the world. This should be the definition of a new world. A world where there is equality not only between races in one nation, but every country across the beautiful and fragile world.

Now, in 2015, it is common for a young boy to be killed before he turns twenty-five years old. It is accepted that a young girl gets pregnant before she turns eighteen years old. For those young children to be posted on that corner to sell a drug, or that baby girl to sell her body. It is not right! That those same children will birth a generation that is worse than they were, because of the lack of knowledge and self-respect. I'm tired of seeing what this world is becoming. I'm afraid to look at where this world will be in ten years. Because if the course and path is not changed for the better, then the bad will only get worse.

There will be so many deaths that the elderly will surpass the amount of youth. The amount of babies will surpass the amount of adult parents to raise them. Then what will the world be, with no young adults with the ability to lead and raise a nation? There will be such a gap, with the elders dying off, and nobody to raise and guide the babies. The world will be no more. The human race will be no more, only extinction, only a lost thought or idea of what was.

The Art Of Conversation

Clear words produces clear understandings. It would be a better outcome to speak and a burden lifted than to be silent and carry it. As I write these words to the tune and melody of my heartbeat, I personally conclude that the voice, your voice can change the outcome. Communication through conversation in today's society is almost as endangered as the polar bear. Imagine the world without the polar bear. Now, imagine the world without conversation. The world, in my opinion, will not be able to survive the obliteration of the art of conversation. To speak. To be heard. To matter. As technology expands, so does this endangered necessity. So today, tomorrow, and the days that follow, I encourage you to speak. Ask someone, "How are you today?" Produce a conversation and notice how pleasant it is to be heard, to be noticed and matter. It does not take much and it is free; to speak with your voice and listen with your ears.

Just as important as it is to speak and be heard, it is just as satisfying to listen and understand. To listen is to care and respect who is speaking. To comprehend their thoughts and concerns; their voice. Just as you would want someone to hear your voice, understand and appreciate your thoughts. As the golden rule states, "Treat others as you would want them to treat you." And that is what life truly boils down to, equality and acceptance. When you allow yourself to listen and engage fully in intelligent conversations you will begin to feel more fulfilled, to become a part of something more. Just think, what someone says to you that is meaningful, how it lingers in your mind and sometimes become a part of your life. Your voice and reasons can have the same impact on someone. It doesn't have to always be about fighting and disagreements. Even if such disagreements arise, they can be dealt with in an appropriate and respectable manner. For it not to progress into a negative conflict that can produce negative and sometimes tragic results.

      Disagreements are a part of nature, and what would life be without them but plain and boring. Then again, it is how we go about situations. Just because someone has a different idea than your own, doesn't mean that they are disrespecting you or consider your point of view and concerns unimportant or unnecessary. The way people are raised and the circumstances that people come in contact with impacts the way they think. But the power of persuasion and conversation can go a long way. People can become "stuck in their ways", but one conversation can change and transform the worst stubborn critic. So, use your words and converse. Become a part of the verbal world and substitute a text for a phone call per day. We have to make a change in every sector of life to create a better world for our children. We absolutely must, because although technology can create positive benefits, too much of it can destroy. To become so dependent on technology can be damaging to one's mind. And once one lose their mind, it is difficult to get it back, although not impossible. But I'm attempting to prevent this crippling era from commencement.

Although, I notice that it already has. I see ten year old children with smartphones and tablets. When I was thirteen I was still required to use my mother's phone or our home phone. I had no desire to have my own cell phone at this point. It didn't even cross my mind, now children are asking for an iphone at their tenth birthday party. I just don't understand it for the life of me. I remember in high school, everybody used to write notes and pass them around during break. Write a respond letter during the next class and pass them off during the next break in the hallway. That was our form of communication. It transformed into text messages maybe my sophomore year. The notes ceased along with the use of the home phone.

Points to Ponder

-
-
-
-
-
-
-
-
-
-
-

Living the Lyrics

Sex, money, guns, drugs and violence. These are the most popular topics when it comes to rap in the music industry. Growing up in the 90's, don't get me wrong I recall some similar tunes as today, but the difference is that it was more to offer. There was "drop it like it's hot" by Juvenile and "Tip Drill" by Nelly. But on the flip side it was Tupac, who rapped some of the same points, but he offered some intelligence in his lyrics. He portrayed knowledge and wisdom but most of all respect for women. Notorious BIG who had a few songs that related to the disastrous topics, also had songs that neglected the points all together and focused on telling stories of how dreams come true. Or Nas, who I believe was a poet with his lyrics. He too may have dipped his feet in the treacherous waters, but the majority of his lyrics were positive messages and something to look up to. Something to inspire those who listened to his music. My final example to respectful lyrics would be that of Common. His lyrics are graceful and acceptable; he too portrays an image worthy of being heard for generations.

I'm sure that someone is thinking, "They rapped about sex, money, drugs, guns and violence too." But I never said that they did not. Yet, they had more to offer than these points alone. All their music is worthy to surpass their physical lives. Tupac and Notorious BIG's physical beings have long ended, but their lyrics have and I believe will continue to live on, as it respectfully should.

Today the only message in lyrics is to become thugs, degrade women, sell drugs, etc. I rarely hear positive messages, something to encourage education or to live a honest and respectful life. The rate of violence, especially amongst African Americans has and continues to increase significantly. It is absolutely ridiculous what time has come to in respect (or lack thereof) to music. I understand and truly believe that music along with television is a way to brainwash society. But in the same sense it's what people turn to, to find a sense of comfort and relaxation. A way to cope and accept certain challenges that they may be going through and I also do this. I have Pandora stations that are on Gospel, Old School Jams, Old School Classics, things of that nature; and I admit I have a Drake and Gucci Mane station. I'm young and I like to get hyped up at certain events. But I don't follow their lyrics as my blueprint to life.

If you don't believe me, turn to the statistics or look outside and listen to the youth. Growing up I remember playing kickball, tag, and going to buy a cup Icee for a quarter. I recall helping a neighbor for $5.00 a day and I was content and satisfied. When we were young in my hood, yes, we were basically poor, but we had our childhood to some extent. Now, children are banging before they hit their teens, having sex and can't read, and dropping out before the 12th grade. There is barely a whole decade between our childhood in the early 2000s and their childhood now. Many of my childhood friends and associates are buried or in jail for years. But I unfortunately witnessed the transformation of destruction.

We used to have a center where we would all go after school. There were dance groups to prepare for the parade and all. There was almost no serious violence amongst my peers. We took out our anger with the basketball not the gun. I remember vividly the day they closed the center and demolished it. Even to this day there's nothing but empty space where our innocence and safety was taken. My peers turned to the streets from that point. I saw innocent boys forced to turn into violent boys and now incarcerated or deceased young men. The young girls that used to sit on the bleachers and create squares with strings and gossip about the boys playing basketball, now have at least one to four children. They turned to sex and drugs and still reside in the same hood, where their children will have the same fate as them. I'm not excluding myself because that would be untruthful if I did. I would be turning my back on where I'm from and on myself. My testimony is on the surface of my life with many more heartbreaking and unbelievable truths. The full story would be a book within itself.

But I always knew that my mind was far better than my circumstance. I always wrote poems and songs and loved reading and watching the news. I always cherished my family, especially my mother and brothers. I knew I had to go to college to make a new path for my family; especially my baby brother Seneca. I refuse to allow him to live a life that I know he's better than. All my other brothers are grown and their life and decisions are theirs. I can only give advice and do everything that I can to lead them. But Seneca is still in high school. I still have to show him that we can and will achieve every ounce of greatness that our ancestors and future generations deserve.

It takes one mind to elevate others. I understand that rappers are referencing what they've been through. But I feel like they should tell the youth what not to do and not to follow their paths and lead them to destruction. People can go down the same path but have completely different outcomes. It would be so much better if the young could listen to it and still manage to live a respectable life that is theirs. But as previously stated the proof is in the pudding if you will. So much of the youth is treating the lyrics as the Bible. Treating these artists as their God and accepting the fate that the lyrics create for them. It's all about controlling your mind and not allowing the influence of others to sway and predict the life you will live. You must be strong minded and strong willed so that you will not become a vulnerable object of the world.

I heard a song the other day and in my opinion it was one of the most detrimental things I've heard coming from a black man. "If I don't do anything in life, I counted money." Really! So when your life is inevitably over is that all that matters. Is that you counted money? Who after you can say that? How many before you? If you have it, do something more, be the person to build a dynasty that can change the face of the world. Because honestly, do you think that your most trusted trustee will bury it with you? Would you? We must come together to create and enforce a better society that will benefit our children significantly.

Deceived Destiny of Destruction

Looking out into the world, many people may believe that our destiny is already set in stone. The increasing number of deaths and violence with hope and respect decreasing at a more rapid pace. I have started to see the amount of gravestones mercifully surpass the amount of birth certificates. People have more hate and resentment in their souls than ever before, in my opinion. It has been an entire era of this ignorance and deceit that is defining the outcome of not only our lives but the lives that has yet to be created.

Lives that may never become into existence because their parents' potential has fallen victim to the planned deception. This is more so for the black race. It has been structured for this race to be weakened and destroyed before we were even able to prove our worth. Beginning way beyond the slavery era, we were viewed as inferior and nothing more than the descendants of monkeys. Of an animal with no mind or no sense of right and wrong. Before we were able to give, it had already long been taken.

Now, today the destruction continues and it is far worse than it used to be, far worse than it should be. I am very strong and firm in my spirituality and I believe sincerely that everything happens for a reason. But I also believe in the power of free will. We have the opportunity to lay the foundation and concrete to a path that will allow us to become victors of this world, of our lives. To stop believing and living the deceit that was created and passed down to destroy us. We have to do better, because the violence against each other is unnecessary. You should not have so much pleasure and thrill from taking the life of another, who's in the same position as you.

A position where they were told that they were never going to amount to anything or ever be good enough. From the tongues that spoke such words, they were told of similar fates. So they can only speak of the lessons they were taught. But what if the negative and degrading sentiments were ignored; and if not ignored, try encouraging. Take the negative words and allow them to build you into someone that the speaker, even yourself never imagined, because it is possible. Possible to allow your mind to transform and excel beyond all depths and heights. Beyond all limitations of this world, better yet, the universe. All it takes is the will to be better. The determination to help lay this foundation of a better road for our future generations. Why must we continue to bury our brothers and cousins and sons because of ignorance?

Testimony

Kenny was going through a very rough time at the time of his passing. Demons had infiltrated his mind and led him down a path of pain and disaster, and ultimately his death. Long story short, one August 18, 2013 he was with his new found "girlfriend" and a "friend". They were to meet up with another guy before reaching their final destination. Once there a struggle began, the "girlfriend" and "friend" did nothing to help my brother as the other guy held a gun to him. He ran before he was shot and killed. Eye witnesses told my family that after this occurred all three went through his pockets as he was fighting for his life. When the cops arrived they "played their part" and the cops never questioned the honest witnesses. It turned out that they had set my brother up because they thought he had money. They killed him to try to take what they thought he had. Yet, all parties involved are still free, because they said it was my brother's gun. And the most important, his murderer was white. This is a commonality in this world today. Racism and inequality is still present although the chains and "colored only" barriers have been removed.

    I could allow this damaging fact to consume me. Allow anger and hatred to take over my being and force me to become something that could ruin and destroy. Yet, I am able to take control of this situation. I could commit sins and break laws toward the parties involved; an act of vigilante and revenge. Take the laws into my own hands since the book is held in the hands of the whites, created by and for them only. But what good would that do? Another life that would become trapped in a system, in which I'm dedicated to discover loopholes? Demolish my brother's memories and desires for me.

    I chose to become great in a world where I'm still viewed as inferior. I choose to live a life that my brother will be proud of. A life where I will bring justice to those involved. But in due time. I choose to write this book, instead of pull the trigger, all because I have much to offer that goes beyond one cell, and three lives.

The Art of Grieving

Everybody deals with the same circumstances differently, the art of grieving to be specific. Pain, disbelief, denial, and regret are some of the many components of grieving. And well, to each their own. But it's more about how you deal with these emotions that matters the most. You can allow the inevitable to consume you and make you fall into depression, or you can breathe, reflect on what has happened, accept that there is no rewinding, and make the best decisions of the worst situations.

I understand. To have so much pain inside your being that you want to drown yourself in the local pond. Trust me, I had the thought numerous times. But you must ask yourself, "What good would that do me?" or "What benefit would that bring my loved ones?" None. You seek a temporary solution, but to up and drown is permanent. It is overwhelming and sometimes overbearing. Some say that with time you will heal. I would never fix my mouth to say, or my hand to write such thing. To lose someone close is a void that will never be filled. Time will not heal the absence of the loved one lost, if anything time will make it harder. The idea that year after year could have been years of birthdays, memories, to become wiser. Better. Time can make it harder to grasp.

So we must train our minds to take another approach. To think of and recall on memories of the time that was shared, to be able to survive on the thought of their smiles and laughs, even their angry and worse days. Instead of simply the thought of "anymore" or "never again". That is the concept and way of thinking the will bring you the most misery. Again, trust me. Now with time, it will get better. With time, all training prevails if taken seriously and appropriately.

Testimony

On August 16, 2013, I was blessed to see 22 years. It was a marvelous and good day although times were rough. My college courses were about to begin, I still had the job I rather enjoyed, and my family and loved ones were together and in good health, or so I thought. The night had come and I was in the process of getting ready to step out with two of my dearest friends when my mother calls. I speak with her for a few moments before my big brother Kenny got on the line. He is going on and on and on about the current female he is seeing. He was speaking in a foreign language that I have never heard him speak before in my life. I should have known something was affecting his mental state right then and there. Because for 22 years my brother only spoke to me with love, admiration and respect. That night, his voice I heard, but he was missing. I didn't want to hear any more of his words so I rushed him off the phone. We said our loves before we hung up. That and the fact that I was able to hear his voice is the reason I am able to at least half way survive.

On August 18, 2013 before my phone rang I was in the process of cleaning my apartment. It was Sunday, I went to church that morning and I was off work. I couldn't ask for a more peaceful day. The icing on the cake was that my boyfriend was gone to football a meeting. So I was literally alone in my mind and space, with the attempt to collect freedom and peace within my spirit. The ring came in maybe around 8pm as I looked down and saw "Mommy" on the caller id. I answered as if it would be a normal conversation, not the conversation that would change my life and the road of my destiny. It was my mother's friend, Hope, who had informed me that Kenny had been shot. I instantly froze and my mind, body and soul went blank. Even so, I believed that he was shot and the wound was non-life threatening. Until she confirmed that he had been shot in the chest. I was already on my knees screaming at this point, but who would hear? I'm home alone. I know that my love has asthma and such an impact would be dangerous. I remember Hope saying that she would call me right back, so I called my boyfriend to tell him the news.

A few moments later I received the call that will haunt my life for the rest of my physical being existence. "He's gone." was her exact words with hope and life missing from her voice. Hope has been a great and dear friend of the family since my senior year of high school in 2009. So I knew she too was hurt by this revelation. But me, I broke before I could run to the restroom and kneel in front of the toilet. I called my boyfriend with the attempt to collect words that could have been understood, to no prevail. He was still at his meeting and couldn't leave at that exact moment, so he sent his friend, who was also a neighbor, to come check on me. I couldn't answer a call, let alone the door. I was paralyzed. And on that day, the world may never know, until now, I tried to commit suicide. As I sat on my bathroom floor, with my boyfriend on the opposite side of the door in the bedroom. I put plastic over my head and began to inhale. Until I couldn't. I laid there with my breathe faint and my thoughts slowly fading. Then to God, I heard No! I sat up as fast as I went down and stared blankly.

Before that night expired I was in Knoxville, Tennessee, more than 300 miles away from where my life had almost slipped. I walked into my mother's house and there she was. Like I've never in my life seen her before. Attempting to write his eulogy with nothing but his name wrote down. Listen, she attempted to write his eulogy only a few hours after his soul was called. I never understood why. However, I knew I had to get to her. It had always been her, Kenny, Seneca and I; throughout the roughest times of our lives, it was us. Now without him? How? Why? I asked and I know she did. We will never get our answers and we will stop asking, because God is God and he makes no mistakes. And to question his actions is to question him. And I can't live my life questioning my God. So we say, "God makes no mistakes and everything happens for a reason and His purpose." That is our answer.

See, I never would have imagined that my big brother would be taken from me. He is the only person in this universe that would listen and understand because he has always been there. Through the fires, the foster homes, the hungry and dark days. Every single dark day and night of my life for 22 years, my brother was with me. He was my person. He is my person. I talk to him with my issues and concerns and he still listens. Because I know exactly what he would say. So in order for me to survive and prevail, I rely on memories. He smiles, his laughs, his soul. I can't allow my mind to slip into a place where I am fixated on the thought of what could have been. Because that is where you will begin to lose yourself. We must all accept what we cannot change, and this is imperative. You must allow such lose to benefit you and make you stronger. If I'd committed suicide that night, his murderer would have took two of my mother's children with one bullet; and that would be worse than one. I survive on the facts that my love constantly told me how proud of me he was and I always know how much my brother love me. Even to this day I know that he is proud and that he wants me to defeat the doubt, anger, pain and resentment in my soul. So that I can become who he always knew I would be. That is the memory that keeps me going.

  We must live strong, so that our loved ones memories may live on strong through us. If we forget and lose who they knew us as, we lose them. The memories of who they were and what they stood for. My brother left behind two adorable baby boys, and for the life of me they will know exactly who their father was. Who he is, because he lives through us. They will look at their grandmother, aunt, and uncles and they will know who their father is.

Thus, we must accept. I know full heartily that it is farthest from easy than the earth and the stars. But it is possible, only if you allow your mind to believe that the possibility exists. Just as God is real, so is Satan and he will destroy you and make you regret the memories that you should cherish. We must make good of such a drastic lose. We must defeat Satan and the demons that try to weaken our minds. Because our minds is one thing that nobody or thing should be able to touch. And remember and believe that it is such a terrible thing to waste.

Faith, Things Unseen

I'm able to write these words, think this manifest by faith. Faith that my thoughts and emotions that created these words will be read and understood by those who opens the cover. I could not be able to see such, even as I write these lines. I have no idea where it will go, anywhere, if beyond my tablet and computer. But my faith is strong and rooted in my belief and desire. In my hopes and dreams that I will be able to motivate this generation and those yet to be created. That is all faith is; evidence of things unseen. Is that not why anybody does anything that they find worthy of doing. They believe that it will be successful and approved. I'm sure someone is thinking "Well, as long as I write what I need to write, or say what I need to say, I don't care if it is approved or not." That may be so, but you do care if it is heard or read. Nobody speaks or writes to be ignored. Regardless of what the individuals may force themselves to believe.

If we believe that our thoughts and concerns will be heard, be understood and accepted, we may begin to speak more, loud, and proud. When we speak we must have faith that the other person is listening; only by faith because they are not obligated to do so. That is one of the main points that I would like to illustrate. Nobody is obligated to do anything that will benefit others. We are not required to take others into consideration. But I ask, wouldn't you? Want others to do things that would benefit you or take you into consideration. I touch again on the golden rule of life, to treat others the way you would want to be treated.

That rule and faith should be the foundation that builds the generations. That defines them in a way and so far that our current living conditions would be seen as a horror movie. A place that they would never want to live. Just as my generation, we are not perfect, but I see how far we have come from segregation. How I would never want to live in times where I must enter through backdoors, or under "Colored Only" signs. I envision my baby nephews listen to our current state and say, "I wouldn't been able to survive during that time." As so many in my generation states now.

As so many fought, spoke, and died to allow us to become integrated and not "free", but have more freedom than before. We can again fight, speak, and sacrifice for this battle that goes beyond a single life. To have a bigger purpose and contribute to the future of a better world. But it begins with the way we think and the way we view others. If we view them as worthy we will be more willing and open to help them thrive; so that they may be more willing to help others.

Before I begin to speak, and understand the power and influence in my words, I am influenced by and respect the quote by Marianne Williamson who said:

"Our deepest fear is not that we are inadequate. Our deepest fear is that we are powerful beyond measure. It is our light, not our darkness that most frightens us. We ask ourselves, Who am I to be brilliant, gorgeous, talented, fabulous? Actually, who are you not to be? You are a child of God. Your playing small does not serve the world. There is nothing enlightened about shrinking so that other people won't feel insecure around you. We are all meant to shine, as children do. We were born to make manifest the glory of God that is within us. It's not just in some of us; it's in everyone. And as we let our own light shine, we unconsciously give other people the right to do the same. As we are liberated from our own fear, our presence automatically liberates others."

Regardless of your religion, God is God and my God is a good God. Burdens, struggles, misfortunes, disaster, and misery is all a part of life. You can say that it comes with the territory. But what one must believe and realize is that none of these trials last always. None of these are permanent factors, unless you allow them to be. This is what I was referring to when I was talking about not allowing your circumstance to determine your outcome. Allowing your mind and faith to come together to raise you above the temporary and deliver you to more permanent situations. Happiness, success, love, satisfaction, and a strong mind are permanent components of life.

Someone wonders how I could say that the positives are permanent yet the negatives doesn't last always. One word and one name that stands alone is all the proof I need on this planet that allows me to believe so. God! He says that if you believe in him and doubt him not, if you put no other God before him, you will reap the benefits of entering into his Kingdom. Which is what? All the positives for eternity! How we live now in our temporary being is what will determine our permanent fate.

Many of us have become comfortable with blaming others for our problems. Even more so, we are so comfortable with placing blame on God because of these shortcomings. But as my preacher once said, "Some of our wounds are created by God, for he will heal you. One cannot be healed without being wounded first." The sermon that day was one of the most powerful that I've had the grace of experiencing. Doesn't it make sense? Imagine as a child, falling off your bike and scraping your knee. Although you felt the pain and burn momentarily you knew that you'd get back on your bike and ride again. You knew that once a bandage was in place for a few days, your wound will begin to close and you would be healed. Because you fell and became wounded you learned how to take pain; you learned the process of being injured and being healed. That instance as a child, is still set as we become adults. The burdens and scares are greater and may have a more powerful impact, but as we were healed from our innocent scares, we too will be healed from these wounds.

You may be surprised if I was to say that the greatest part of being healed is not that fact in itself. But the fact that there will be no evidence of what you've been through. By viewing me without reading my testimony, honestly, how much would you have guessed? Nowhere near as much I would assume. Because all those wounds has been healed, and I am smiling because it is over. That storm that clouded my life thus, my mind for years has been removed by beautiful and glorious sunshine. It's not always such a bad thing to act brand new. I testify that I am brand new. You see, I don't walk like I used to walk. I don't talk like I used to talk. I don't think the way I used to think. Because I have grown and changed, and change is sometimes good. You may recall this verse from the Bible,

"When I was a child, I talked like a child, I thought like a child, I reasoned like a child. But when I became an adult, I set aside childish ways." -1 Cor, 13:11 Now, if that doesn't make you feel something, ask yourself would someone in childish ways find it reasoning?

Once you begin to grow, really grow, and I don't mean age by any means; for I know of thirty year old children. But mentally to the point where you are able to improve your life simply by thinking of better solutions. That is when you have set your childish ways aside. A child has not yet gained enough years, let alone experience to understand the difference. But as adults we have, and must remain sober and aware so that we will share revelations to our youth that will encourage them. For your words, your thoughts and experiences can change the path others may take.

We must teach them about faith and about making a way for themselves through hard work. Many people are so quick to try to rob someone of their belongings, forgetting that we all struggle.

"Be sober and alert. Your enemy the devil, like a roaring lion, is on the prowl looking for someone to devour. Resist him. Stay strong in your faith because you know that your brothers and sisters throughout the world are enduring the same kinds of suffering." - 1 Peter 5:8-9

Regardless of your living situations and finances, this life on earth has promised nothing but suffering. But it is how you handle such burdens that matter. You can own all your desires and possess every plate of gold on earth. But I guarantee that you will have some form of burden and suffering, just as the poor man. Although they differ, there's many types of struggles, in which we each have. Yet, we can have mental control over these situations, therefore, you will have complete control.

Inheritance

To inherit something can mean so many different things. To receive something when someone dies, to receive characteristics from a parent, etc. But for this instance, I will define inheritance as meaning: to possess something that has been passed down from generations. We have inherited the burden of being viewed as inferior and "something" less than peasantry. As "something" who is not able to be brilliant and incredible. Some still see me as "something" who should be on my knees and sweating in the cotton fields. But that is not the case. Through our ancestry and our past we have inherited strength and the will to survive. We cannot allow people to define us and what we've overcome who has not been in our shoes.

There has been many that stood and fought to give us the chance to become more than what "they" wanted us to be. "People are not born hating someone because of the color of their skin" as stated by the late Nelson Mandela. They are taught and learn to hate and judge those who are different. But just as hate can be instilled so can love, for love is a more natural emotion derived from the heart. I can believe that we can change the face of the world, by instilling goodness into the lives of our children, our future. We can show them how to live in a world without violence and hate. Being enlightened will take place as the world is different from the days of slavery. New ideals should be formed and placed that can serve all people equally. It should be so, that if one murders he should be rightfully punished.

Violence has to cease and the negative influences that promote such violence should be ignored and condemned. Positivity should thrive and respect for others shall one day prevail. How many more brothers should we bury? Mothers should cry and children should be raised without a parent. Only to become what created their fate and take another? Why is such cycle accepted? For how many generations, must this continue, before our eyes are opened? How many more children should be denied a life, children be denied a father or mother due to ignorance and violence.

I am tired of the constant increase in murders of brothers at the hand of their brother, whose ancestors picked the same cotton and bowed to the same white man. My heart breaks at the horrid fact that nobody views this as a disaster that has to stop. But I believe that my heart will soon be healed.

Last Word

The mind leads the body while the body takes the journey. So, what is a journey without a mind? It isn't hard to achieve the goal. It isn't difficult to be positive and live a healthy life. It only takes the will and some exercise. But the benefit will be grand and you will be fulfilled. Believe in your faith and believe in your mind. In you. And together we will Cherish Prosperity.

Acknowledgements

God: First and foremost it is He who I give all my praise. For his name stands alone. What would I be without his grace, mercy, forgiveness, love and guidance. Nowhere. So for these reasons and his blessings of my life. I give all glory to God.

My queen: My reason, my heart, my mother, LaTonya Pullens. Thank you for being a mother through countless obstacles and never once abandoning me or my brothers. Your strength continues as you raise Kenny's children. It amazes me how your faith and love never wavers. I dedicate who I am to you solely. Period.

Brothers: William, Devonta, and D'tearius Southern. Seneca Oden Jr, Christopher Bell and Angelo Gleaves. I thank you all for loving me unconditionally and creating some of the happiest moments in my life. Thank you all for encouraging me and believing in my ability. I love you all tremendously.

Sisters: Tiesha McKenzie, Kristin Riddle, Nicole Hatmaker and Aissa McMurray. Thank you all for the love and support throughout countless years. Blood played no factor in our sisterhood bond. But it couldn't make us any closer.

Franklin: My king on earth. Thank you. You are truly a great man and I love you purely. You have been nothing less than supportive since my first word was written. It was only God that brought you to my life. I love you and this is dedicated to you. I love you my hazel eyed king.

Friends: So many to name, but you know who you are. I thank you for the constant support. Thank you for your motivation and love. I appreciate the times you took to read my words. I will never be able to express my truest and deepest gratitude. Thank You All!

My Angel

My dedication to you. Thank you. Words can never express the amount of love that I have for you. You have always been my best friend and my true soul mate. You are the funniest and sweetest person that I've ever had the blessing of loving. It's still surreal. You know. But I accept God's plan. Because you are with me 100 percent every day. You are a great father, amazing son, marvelous brother, astounding grandson, and outstanding friend. Thank you so much for blessing me with two life lines. Ke'lonzo "Deon" Pullens and LaVonta "Tay" Pullens are your exact image. And for that I am thankful. I have you in the heavens and on earth. I have you everywhere. I love you and I miss you Kenny. For the rest of my life.

Pledge

I, _____, pledge to take the necessary steps to Mind Elevation. I will instill knowledge and positive energy in those around me. I will think of positive outcomes to all negative situations. I will instill positive messages and create a positive life for the children in my life. I pledge to take my part in changing lives. On my honor, I will help in Chasing Prosperity!

About The Author

Chanekka "Chae'" Pullens currently resides in Murfreesboro, Tn where she attends Middle Tennessee State University. She plans on receiving her Bachelors Degree in Political Science with a double minor in International Relations and History in August 2015. After receiving her degree, she plans to travel across the nation to promote Mind Elevation.

www.ingramcontent.com/pod-product-compliance
Lightning Source LLC
Chambersburg PA
CBHW031209090426
42736CB00009B/847